The Essential Buyer's Guide

Porsche
986 BOXSTER

Boxster, Boxster S, Boxster S 550 Spyder
Model years 1997 to 2005

Your marque expert:
Adrian Streather

VELOCE PUBLISHING
THE PUBLISHER OF FINE AUTOMOTIVE BOOKS

The Essential Buyer's Guide Series

Alfa Romeo Alfasud (Metcalfe)
Alfa Romeo Alfetta: all saloon/sedan models 1972 to 1984 & coupé
models 1974 to 1987 (Metcalfe)
Alfa Romeo Giulia GT Coupé (Booker)
Alfa Romeo Giulia Spider (Booker)
Audi TT (Davies)
Audi TT Mk2 2006 to 2014 (Durnan)
Austin-Healey Big Healeys (Trummel)
BMW Boxer Twins (Henshaw)
BMW E30 3 Series 1981 to 1994 (Hosier)
BMW GS (Henshaw)
BMW X5 (Saunders)
BMW Z3 Roadster (Fishwick)
BMW Z4: E85 Roadster and E86 Coupé including M and Alpina 2003 to
2009 (Smitheram)
BSA 350, 441 & 500 Singles (Henshaw)
BSA 500 & 650 Twins (Henshaw)
BSA Bantam (Henshaw)
Choosing, Using & Maintaining Your Electric Bicycle (Henshaw)
Citroën 2CV (Paxton)
Citroën DS & ID (Heilig)
Cobra Replicas (Ayre)
Corvette C2 Sting Ray 1963-1967 (Falconer)
Datsun 240Z 1969 to 1973 (Newlyn)
DeLorean DMC-12 1981 to 1983 (Williams)
Ducati Bevel Twins (Falloon)
Ducati Desmodue Twins (Falloon)
Ducati Desmoquattro Twins – 851, 888, 916, 996, 998, ST4 1988 to 2004
(Falloon)
Fiat 500 & 600 (Bobbitt)
Ford Capri (Paxton)
Ford Escort Mk1 & Mk2 (Williamson)
Ford Focus RS/ST 1st Generation (Williamson)
Ford Model A – All Models 1927 to 1931 (Buckley)
Ford Model T – All models 1909 to 1927 (Barker)
Ford Mustang – First Generation 1964 to 1973 (Cook)
Ford Mustang – Fifth Generation (2005-2014) (Cook)
Ford RS Cosworth Sierra & Escort (Williamson)
Harley-Davidson Big Twins (Henshaw)
Hillman Imp (Morgan)
Hinckley Triumph triples & fours 750, 900, 955, 1000, 1050, 1200 – 1991-
2009 (Henshaw)
Honda CBR FireBlade (Henshaw)
Honda CBR600 Hurricane (Henshaw)
Honda SOHC Fours 1969-1984 (Henshaw)
Jaguar E-Type 3.8 & 4.2 litre (Crespin)
Jaguar E-type V12 5.3 litre (Crespin)
Jaguar Mark 1 & 2 (All models including Daimler 2.5-litre V8) 1955 to 1969
(Thorley)
Jaguar New XK 2005-2014 (Thorley)
Jaguar S-Type – 1999 to 2007 (Thorley)
Jaguar X-Type – 2001 to 2009 (Thorley)
Jaguar XJ-S (Crespin)
Jaguar XJ6, XJ8 & XJR (Thorley)
Jaguar XK 120, 140 & 150 (Thorley)
Jaguar XK8 & XKR (1996-2005) (Thorley)
Jaguar/Daimler XJ 1994-2003 (Crespin)
Jaguar/Daimler XJ40 (Crespin)
Jaguar/Daimler XJ6, XJ12 & Sovereign (Crespin)
Kawasaki Z1 & Z900 (Orritt)
Land Rover Discovery Series 1 (1989-1998) (Taylor)
Land Rover Discovery Series 2 (1998-2004) (Taylor)
Land Rover Series I, II & IIA (Thurman)
Land Rover Series III (Thurman)
Lotus Elan, S1 to Sprint and Plus 2 to Plus 2S 130/5 1962 to 1974 (Vale)
Lotus Europa, S1, S2, Twin-cam & Special 1966 to 1975 (Vale)
Lotus Seven replicas & Caterham 7: 1973-2013 (Hawkins)
Mazda MX-5 Miata (Mk1 1989-97 & Mk2 98-2001) (Crook)
Mazda RX-8 (Parish)
Mercedes-Benz 190: all 190 models (W201 series) 1982 to 1993 (Parish)
Mercedes-Benz 280-560SL & SLC (Bass)
Mercedes-Benz G-Wagen (Greene)

Mercedes-Benz Pagoda 230SL, 250SL & 280SL roadsters & coupés
(Bass)
Mercedes-Benz S-Class W126 Series (Zoporowski)
Mercedes-Benz S-Class Second Generation W116 Series (Parish)
Mercedes-Benz SL R129-series 1989 to 2001 (Parish)
Mercedes-Benz SLK (Bass)
Mercedes-Benz W123 (Parish)
Mercedes-Benz W124 – All models 1984-1997 (Zoporowski)
MG Midget & A-H Sprite (Horler)
MG TD, TF & TF1500 (Jones)
MGA 1955-1962 (Crosier)
MGB & MGB GT (Williams)
MGF & MG TF (Hawkins)
Mini (Paxton)
Morgan Plus 4 (Benfield)
Morris Minor & 1000 (Newell)
Moto Guzzi 2-valve big twins (Falloon)
New Mini (Collins)
Norton Commando (Henshaw)
Peugeot 205 GTI (Blackburn)
Piaggio Scooters – all modern two-stroke & four-stroke automatic models
1991 to 2016 (Willis)
Porsche 356 (Johnson)
Porsche 911 (964) (Streather)
Porsche 911 (991) (Streather)
Porsche 911 (993) (Streather)
Porsche 911 (996) (Streather)
Porsche 911 (997) – Model years 2004 to 2009 (Streather)
Porsche 911 (997) – Second generation models 2009 to 2012 (Streather)
Porsche 911 Carrera 3.2 (Streather)
Porsche 911SC (Streather)
Porsche 924 – All models 1976 to 1988 (Hodgkins)
Porsche 928 (Hemmings)
Porsche 930 Turbo & 911 (930) Turbo (Streather)
Porsche 944 (Higgins)
Porsche 981 Boxster & Cayman (Streather)
Porsche 986 Boxster (Streather)
Porsche 987 Boxster and Cayman 1st generation
(2005-2009) (Streather)
Porsche 987 Boxster and Cayman 2nd generation (2009-2012) (Streather)
Range Rover – First Generation models 1970 to 1996 (Taylor)
Range Rover – Second Generation 1994-2001 (Taylor)
Range Rover – Third Generation L322 (2002-2012) (Taylor)
Reliant Scimitar GTE (Payne)
Rolls-Royce Silver Shadow & Bentley T-Series (Bobbitt)
Rover 2000, 2200 & 3500 (Marrocco)
Royal Enfield Bullet (Henshaw)
Subaru Impreza (Hobbs)
Sunbeam Alpine (Barker)
Triumph 350 & 500 Twins (Henshaw)
Triumph Bonneville (Henshaw)
Triumph Herald & Vitesse (Ayre)
Triumph Spitfire and GT6 (Ayre)
Triumph Stag (Mort)
Triumph Thunderbird, Trophy & Tiger (Henshaw)
Triumph TR2 & TR3 - All models (including 3A & 3B) 1953 to 1962
(Conners)
Triumph TR4/4A & TR5/250 - All models 1961 to 1968 (Child & Battyll)
Triumph TR6 (Williams)
Triumph TR7 & TR8 (Williams)
Triumph Trident & BSA Rocket III (Rooke)
TVR Chimaera and Griffith (Kitchen)
TVR S-series (Kitchen)
Velocette 350 & 500 Singles 1946 to 1970 (Henshaw)
Vespa Scooters – Classic 2-stroke models 1960-2008 (Paxton)
Volkswagen Bus (Copping)
Volkswagen Transporter T4 (1990-2003) (Copping/Cservenka)
VW Golf GTI (Copping)
VW Beetle (Copping)
Volvo 700/900 Series (Beavis)
Volvo P1800/1800S, E & ES 1961 to 1973 (Murray)

www.veloce.co.uk

First published in September 2012, reprinted October 2016, December 2017 and November 2019 by Veloce Publishing Limited, Veloce House, Parkway Farm
Business Park, Middle Farm Way, Poundbury, Dorchester, Dorset, DT1 3AR, England.
Tel 01305 260068/fax 01305 250479/e-mail info@veloce.co.uk/web www.veloce.co.uk or www.velocebooks.com.

ISBN: 978-1-787116-54-2 UPC: 6-36847-01654-8

© Adrian Streather and Veloce Publishing 2012, 2016, 2017 & 2019. All rights reserved. With the exception of quoting brief passages for the purpose of review, no
part of this publication may be recorded, reproduced or transmitted by any means, including photocopying, without the written permission of Veloce Publishing
Ltd. Throughout this book logos, model names and designations, etc, have been used for the purposes of identification, illustration and decoration. Such names
are the property of the trademark holder as this is not an official publication.
Readers with ideas for automotive books, or books on other transport or related hobby subjects, are invited to write to the editorial director of Veloce Publishing at
the above address.
British Library Cataloguing in Publication Data – A catalogue record for this book is available from the British Library.
Typesetting, design and page make-up all by Veloce Publishing Ltd on Apple Mac. Printed and Bound by CPI Group (UK) Ltd, Croydon, CR04YY.

Introduction
– the purpose of this book

The information in this buyer's guide is arranged in user-friendly chapters to allow any prospective purchaser of a road legal Porsche 986 Boxster to make informed decisions on whether to proceed, or not, with a purchase after viewing and test driving a specific car.

Anyone considering purchasing a mid-engine Porsche 986 Boxster should be aware of some negative reaction to the model created by those who despise any Porsche fitted with a water-cooled engine. "It's not a real Porsche" are words commonly heard by Boxster owners, even though it wears the brand's badge on the front luggage compartment lid.

The 986 Boxster was Porsche's first entry level product since the 924 rolled off the line at the Neckarsulm VW/Audi factory in model year 1976. The Porsche 924 with its 2.0-litre Audi water-cooled engine was a huge sales success. 21 model years later Porsche launched a two-seat, mid-engine, 2.5-litre, water-cooled roadster named the '986 Boxster' into the entry level sports car market, and it, too, was an instant success. However, amongst the air-cooled Porsche purists it was not liked, and they created a furore much like that unleashed by Porsche 356 owners when that model was replaced by the 901/911 series in model year 1964, or when the water-cooled 911 (996) model range was developed. It's not possible to unravel the Boxster myths and legends that abound on the internet in just a few pages. So what's true?

The Boxster M96.20/21/22/23/24 engine series has had some issues. Cracked bores (followed by a failed fix by Porsche when it inserted cylinder sleeves in a limited number of 2.5-litre M96.20 engines and the sleeves started to slip); failed intermediate shaft bearings; contaminated coolant via failed oil-water heat exchangers; leaking rear main crankshaft seal. Sadly, the way these issues were dealt with by the manufacturer (no comment) quickly magnified these problems into one of the worst public relations exercises in history. However, Boxster sales never suffered as a consequence (see chapter 17).

Like the Porsche 928, the 986 Boxster was never factory-prepared for motor racing and, again like the 928, it has developed its own worldwide enthusiast base. The model also attracted the attention of manufacturer and tuner RUF Automobile and other tuning companies such as Gemballa, TechArt and Strosek who all produced tuned versions.

The 986 Boxster series was produced over nine model years with total combined production from Germany and Finland reaching 164,874 units. It came with three different engines, 2.5, 2.7 and 3.2 litres in three different flavours; Boxster, Boxster S and Boxster S 550 Spyder 50th Anniversary Edition (1964 cars built in model year 2004 only). It was only manufactured as two-seat Roadster with an electric fabric folding roof (rag top), but a lightweight hardtop was available for all models.

Owning a pre-loved 986 Boxster, Boxster S or Boxster 550 Spyder can provide years of motoring pleasure and enjoyment from being part of the Porsche experience.

The only way a 986 Boxster purchase can potentially ruin the Porsche experience is if it suffers a catastrophic engine failure which, whilst rare, is not very amusing. However, a full repair or even a factory (dealer supplied) exchange engine is no more expensive than an overhaul of a flat-six air-cooled engine, and much cheaper than a new air-cooled engine in most countries.

Special thanks to all credited photographic contributors mentioned in this book.

The Porsche 924 was Porsche AG's first true worldwide entry level product attempt. (Author collection)

The last 986 Boxster rolled off the line in model year 2005. (Courtesy Porsche AG archive)

RUF-tuned and painted 986 Boxster. The special paint changes colour with the light. (Author collection)

Contents

The Essential Buyer's Guide™ currency
At the time of publication a BG unit of currency "●" equals approximately £1.00/US$1.22/Euro 1.11. Please adjust to suit current exchange rates using Sterling as the base currency.

1 Is it the right Porsche for you?
– marriage guidance

Tall and short drivers
All 986 Boxster models, left- and right-hand drive, provide a comfortable driving position for short and tall drivers as an adjustable position steering wheel is installed and there's plenty of seat adjustment as it's a true two-seater.

Weight of controls
All 986 Boxster models are fitted with power steering, which helps to significantly reduce loads on the driver's arms. All are fitted with a very effective vacuum brake boost system, and the hydraulic clutch operating system is lighter to operate with far less stress on the left leg than with previous Porsche series.

Will it fit the garage?
Chapter 17 contains a table with specific model dimensions. Measure your garage and compare, but don't forget the car's doors have to be opened in the garage.

Interior space
There's plenty of leg room in the 986 Boxster for both driver and passenger. Comfort does depend on type of seat installed. The standard comfort seat nicely supports people of average girth, but the optional sports seat is just that little bit more comfortable (big bit in author's opinion) as it grips one's hips.

Luggage capacity
The Porsche Boxster is a genuine two-seat Roadster meaning that inside the 'office' there not much room for more than the driver and passenger and a few knick knacks. However, because the engine is mounted in the middle the 986 has a front and rear luggage compartment, each capable of carrying a suitcase. A little room is lost in the front luggage compartment because that's where the collapsible spare wheel and tyre assembly is installed.

Running costs
The 986 Boxster cost of ownership in every area is lower than its air-cooled and water-cooled 911 relatives. However, it's still a powerful sports car designed to be driven and the resulting cost of ownership is higher than for a standard road car.

Usability
It's a sports car and I do not recommend the 986 Boxster be driven on snow and ice covered roads, even with proper winter tyres and any other installed safety systems such as the Porsche Stability Management (PSM) introduced as an option in model year 2001. Even the first 2.5-litre-powered Boxster is too powerful and its ride too low for harsh conditions. Plus the salt used in winter will eat away the metal work.

Parts availability
To date no issues related to parts availability have been reported, even for the first model year 1997 production run.

Parts cost
It's a Porsche sports car; expect parts to be relatively expensive.

Insurance
Check with your insurance company, as a 986 Boxster can be expensive to fully insure. If you cannot afford full insurance coverage, you shouldn't purchase one of these cars.

Investment potential
The 986 Boxster offers excellent best bang for your buck in the entry level sports car market, but do not expect to make a profit on resale.

Foibles
Rear main crankshaft seal leak issue took far too long to solve. Carrying out DIY (home) internal engine and transmission repairs is very difficult, if not impossible. It has a neutral feeling in the handling department, not edgy.

986 Boxster front and rear luggage compartments. (Courtesy Porsche AG archive)

Plus points
Every girl loves a Porsche and in the case of the 986 Boxster it's almost love at first sight. Where the 911 series often appeals to the female passenger species the Boxster attracts many more of the female driver species. Ownership costs are lower than for its 911 relatives. It's lighter, faster, better handling and more reliable than most entry level sports cars.

Minus points
Virulent anti-986 Boxster forces at work. Patchy customer support from Porsche AG. Some engine reliability issues such as oil leaking from the engine's rear main crankshaft seal. Navigation system CD and DVD database upgrades discontinued. Hardtop required for wet and cold weather. Boxster S 550 Spyder only has "Boxster S" script on rear luggage compartment.

Alternatives
Porsche Cayman, Mazda MX-5 Miata, Mini Cooper S, BMW Z3, BMW Z4, Mercedes SLK and Honda S2000.

2 Cost considerations
– affordable, or a money pit?

Service by an approved Porsche dealer
Intervals: 12,000 miles/20,000km (small) and 24,000 miles/40,000km (large). Small service cost: from ●x299. Large service cost: from ●x600.

Mechanical parts cost
Rebuilt 2.5- and 2.7-litre M96.20/22/23 engines: from ●x 4250
Rebuilt 3.2-litre M96.21/24 engines: from ●x4250
Full Autofarm (1973) Ltd Silsleeve engine upgrade: ●x6750
Rebuilt G86.00/01/20 manual transmissions: from ●x2500

Simple DIY (do-it-yourself) servicing reduces ownership costs considerably.
(Courtesy Autofarm (1973) Ltd)

Rebuilt A86.00/05/20 Tiptronic transmissions: from ●x3000
Exchange (ex-Porsche) 2.5- and 2.7-litre M96 engine: from ●x8415
Exchange (Porsche) 3.2-litre M96 engine: from ●x7913
Radiator: from ●x110 ea.
Clutch kit: from ●x175 (kit and fitting by Porsche dealer from ●x1100)
Steel cross-drilled brake discs (rotors) front (pair): ●x262
Steel cross-drilled brake discs (rotors) rear (pair): ●x286
Brake pads front (pair): ●x60
Brake pads rear (pair): ●x75
ABS hydraulic unit: ●x1825
Front windscreen wiper arm assemblies (pair): ●x67
Front wiper blades (pair): ●x22

Electronic and electrical parts cost
Alternator: from ●x350
ABS control unit (all): from ●x1132
Heating and air-conditioning control unit: ●x161
Engine control unit (DME) for all engine capacities and types: ●x1862
Tiptronic transmission control unit: ●x1360
Porsche Communication Management PCM-1 (8-bit): from ●x400
Porsche Communication Management 8-bit to 16-bit upgrade: from ●x1200
Porsche Communication Management PCM-2: from ●x2000
Window electric motor: ●x155
Rear spoiler drive motor: ●x692
Headlight: from ●x160
Battery (80 amp/hr) ●x133

Structural work cost

LHD to RHD conversion: Don't even consider it!
Complete body restoration: from ●x15,000
New bodyshell: Price on application from local Porsche dealer
Full repaint (including preparation): from ●x5000
Full professional restoration from basket case: from ●x25,000

Manuals

Factory workshop manual set: from ●x1720 to 5200
Original 986 Boxster owner's manual set: ●x200
PCM-1 (8-bit) navigation CD set: ●x125 (last upgrade 2002)
PCM-1 (16-bit) navigation CD (7) set: ●x500 (last upgrade 2007)
PCM-2 navigation DVD: from ●x150

Parts that are easy to find

At the time of writing the overwhelming majority of 986 Boxster parts are easily obtained from your local factory-approved dealer or independent Porsche parts supplier.

Parts that are hard to find

Porsche Communication Management PCM-1 16-bit navigation unit.
Post model year 2002 glass rear window.
Replacement hardtop.

Parts that are very expensive

Replacement engines and transmission units.
Porsche part number replacement.
Litronic headlight system.
Replacement hardtop.
Fabric for rag top.

Optional Porsche communication management (PCM) system.
(Courtesy Porsche AG archive)

Hardtop is needed for the really cold and wet weather. (Author collection)

3 Living with a 986 Boxster
– will you get along together?

Purchasing any Porsche model is going to have an impact on your entire family and, like its ancestors, the 986 Boxster is not a family car. It was designed for high-speed driving through the Swiss Alps or hurtling down the German Autobahn, French Autoroute, Italian Autostrada, American Highway, Australian Freeway, UK Motorway and anywhere else in the world that has quality high speed roads or major twisty bits. And the mid-engine Boxster is much better than its air-cooled relatives at sitting in heavy traffic because it's water-cooled.

At the time of writing, the youngest 986 Boxster available in most parts of the world is six years old and the oldest fourteen. The good news is that 986 Boxster still makes an excellent daily driver, however bear in mind that adding commuter miles and engine operating time will depreciate the car's future resale value.

The 986 Boxster is an experience to be enjoyed, but does it genuinely fit into your current lifestyle? Do you have a family? The 986 Boxster is a big boy's or girl's toy. It's sometimes referred to as a mid-life crisis fun machine designed for two consenting adults to enjoy in the fast lane. Being a two-seat Roadster with a soft top (rag top) it was never meant to be anything but what it is: an entry level Porsche sports car built for enjoyment rather than practicality.

Are you prepared to look after the 986 Boxster? As with any thoroughbred it needs tender loving care, and it's not the type of car which can be started, driven off seconds later, parked after a short drive and then the process started again. Sufficient warm-up time has to be given to allow the oil, transmission fluid and coolant to start flowing.

There are many electronic systems on the 986 Boxster that need time to run through self-test routines before the car's driven off.

What about exhaust noise? Is it going to impact your family or your neighbours, or attract the attention of local law enforcement? A standard 986 Boxster is certainly quieter than other Porsche model series; but it's still got a very distinct and noticeable sound about it, and is louder than the average people carrier.

What about the money? You can afford to purchase a 986 Boxster, but can you afford to own one? Are you prepared to pay the cost of ensuring the 986 Boxster is always in peak safe, roadworthy condition?

Are you prepared to purchase original parts? Are you prepared to pay a little more (not always the case with all tyre brands) to fit Porsche approved N-rated tyres?

The purchase of any 986 Boxster, be it original Porsche manufactured or tuned by one of the experts like RUF Automobile, will impact your lifestyle, family and wallet: however, the Porsche experience of the 986 Boxster is worth every penny. The 986 Boxster still turns many heads amongst the general public. It's not 'a hairdresser's' car, James May (Captain slow) of *Top Gear* fame owns one, and that's got to mean something, hasn't it?

Why do you want one of these? In this case a 986 Boxster S delivered to Australia. (Courtesy Ken Anson)

RUF Automobile-tuned 986 Boxster. (Author collection)

The 986 Boxster in the 'twisty bits.' (Courtesy Porsche AG archive)

The first questions that must be asked are either prefixed with: "What choices are there?" Or "What do I want?" When it comes to the Porsche 986 Boxster series the choices are somewhat limited.

There are the model years 1997 to 2001 inclusive 2.5-litre Boxster, 2.7-litre Boxster & 3.2-litre Boxster S.

Then there's model year 2002 (known as the face-lift model year) 2.7-litre Boxster, 3.2-litre Boxster S and the model year 2004 Boxster S 550 Spyder (only 1964 built) 50th Anniversary Edition. The Spyder model is an uprated Boxster S with special options and the model script on the rear luggage compartment lid is "Boxster S."

All 2.5- and 2.7-litre Boxster models are either fitted with a five-speed manual or the optional five-speed Tiptronic S (automatic) transmission and were only manufactured in the two-seat roadster body style with rear wheel drive.

The 3.2-litre Boxster S models and the 550 Spyder are fitted with a six-speed manual or optional five-speed Tiptronic S (automatic) transmission, and were also only manufactured in the two-seat roadster body style with rear wheel drive.

Relative values between models is difficult to calculate as any accurate comparison must include variables such as national variant, exterior and interior colour combination, interior materials, solid or metallic paint, options, aftermarket modifications, condition, engine hours, mileage and whether it's a pre-face-lift model range (model years 1997 to 2001) or one of the face-lift model range (model years 2002 to 2005).

Approximate 986 Boxster model relative values are calculated using a datum point of 100% given to the most commonly available version which is the model year 2001 2.7-litre Porsche 986 Boxster with five-speed Tiptronic S transmission.

Model year 1997 2.5-litre Boxster with five-speed manual	80%
Model year 1997 2.5-litre Boxster with five-speed Tiptronic	85%
Model year 1998 2.5-litre Boxster with five-speed manual	80%
Model year 1998 2.5-litre Boxster with five-speed Tiptronic	85%
Model year 1999 2.5-litre Boxster with five-speed manual	85%
Model year 1999 2.5-litre Boxster with five-speed Tiptronic	90%
Model year 2000 2.7-litre Boxster with five-speed manual	95%
Model year 2000 2.7-litre Boxster with five-speed Tiptronic	100%
Model year 2000 3.2-litre Boxster S with six-speed manual	105%
Model year 2000 3.2-litre Boxster S with six-speed Tiptronic	110%
Model year 2001 2.7-litre Boxster with five-speed manual	95%
Model year 2001 2.7-litre Boxster with five-speed Tiptronic	100%
Model year 2001 3.2-litre Boxster S with six-speed manual	105%
Model year 2001 3.2-litre Boxster S with six-speed Tiptronic	110%
Model year 2002 2.7-litre Boxster with five-speed manual	100%
Model year 2002 2.7-litre Boxster with five-speed Tiptronic	105%
Model year 2002 3.2-litre Boxster S with six-speed manual	110%
Model year 2002 3.2-litre Boxster S with six-speed Tiptronic	115%

Model year 2003 2.7-litre Boxster with five-speed manual   110%
Model year 2003 2.7-litre Boxster with five-speed Tiptronic   115%
Model year 2003 3.2-litre Boxster S with six-speed manual   120%
Model year 2003 3.2-litre Boxster S with six-speed Tiptronic   125%
Model year 2004 550 Spyder with 6-speed manual   135%
Model year 2004 2.7-litre Boxster with five-speed manual   110%
Model year 2004 2.7-litre Boxster with five-speed Tiptronic   115%
Model year 2004 3.2-litre Boxster S with six-speed manual   120%
Model year 2004 3.2-litre Boxster S with six-speed Tiptronic   125%
Model year 2005 2.7-litre Boxster with five-speed manual   115%
Model year 2005 2.7-litre Boxster with five-speed Tiptronic   120%
Model year 2005 3.2-litre Boxster S with six-speed manual   125%
Model year 2005 3.2-litre Boxster S with six-speed Tiptronic   130%

Original Porsche 986 Boxster prototype
was first presented in 1993. (Courtesy
Porsche AG archive)

Model year 1997 2.5-litre Boxster.
(Courtesy Porsche AG archive)

Model year 2000
986 Boxster
S. (Courtesy
Porsche AG
archive)

Glass rear window was
introduced in model year 2003.
(Courtesy Russ Standage)

Pre-face-lift (model years
1997 to 2001) 986 Boxster.
(Courtesy Porsche AG archive)

Model year 2001 986 Boxster with
Porsche Exclusive aerokit and sports
package. (Courtesy Porsche AG archive)

Face-lift (model years 2002 to 2005) 986
Boxster S. (Courtesy Russ Standage)

Model year 2001 986 Boxster fitted with
Porsche Exclusive Speedster aerokit.
(Courtesy Porsche AG archive)

One of the last. Model year 2005 986
Boxster S. (Courtesy Porsche AG
archive)

5 Before you view
– be well informed

The key to a successful purchase is research! To avoid a wasted journey it will help if you're very clear about what questions you want to ask before you pick up the telephone. Some of these points might appear basic, but when you're excited about the prospect of buying your dream car it's amazing how some of the most obvious things slip the mind.

Check the current values of the model in which you are interested in car magazines that provide price guides and even auction results.

Where is the car?
Is it going to be worth travelling to the next county, state or even another country? A locally advertised car, although it may not sound very interesting, can add to your knowledge for very little effort, so make a visit – it might even be in better condition than expected.

Dealer or private sale?
Establish early on if the car is being sold by its owner or by a trader. A private owner should have all the history, so don't be afraid to ask detailed questions. A dealer may have more limited knowledge of a car's history, but should have some documentation. A dealer may offer a warranty/guarantee (ask for a printed copy) and finance. Private sales = no warranty and all legal liability on the purchaser's shoulders. Cost of collection and delivery? A dealer will be used to quoting for delivery using car transporters. A private owner may agree to meet you halfway, but only after you have seen the car at the vendor's address to validate the documents. Conversely, you could meet halfway and agree the sale but insist on meeting at the vendor's address for the handover.

View – when and where?
It is always preferable to view at the vendor's home or business premises. In the case of a private sale, the car's documentation must tally with the vendor's name and address. Arrange to view only in daylight and avoid wet days (most cars look better in poor light or when wet).

Reason for sale?
Do make it one of the first questions. Why is the car being sold and how long has it been with the current owner? How many previous owners? Left-hand drive and right-hand drive models are available as Porsche manufactured its model range to comply with individual national requirements. There are nations with right-hand drive regulations that allow local registration of left-hand drive cars, but if left-hand drive is not permitted and private right-hand drive imports are restricted or banned, then a third party conversion may be your only choice, but explore all other avenues first.

Condition (body/chassis/interior/mechanicals)
Ask for an honest appraisal of the car's condition. Ask specifically about some of the check items described in chapter 7. A full systems check and test drive is

mandatory. A completely original 986 Boxster's value is invariably higher than one with aftermarket modifications except the professionally tuned versions (think of the standard market price for the model and start by doubling it to get into the basic ballpark).

Matching data/legal ownership/documentation

It's mandatory for any potential purchaser to ensure the VIN, engine number and licence plate (if applicable) matches the official registration documentation. Is the owner's name and address recorded in the official registration documents? For those countries that require roadworthiness inspections such as an MOT certificate in the UK, or Fahrzeugausweis in Germany (TÜV) and Switzerland (MFK), does the car have a document showing it complies? If an exhaust and/or noise emissions certificate is mandatory, does the car have one? Does the car carry a current road tax or equivalent type sticker, or tag, as required in numerous countries such as the UK and Germany? Does the vendor own the car outright? Money might be owed to a finance company or bank: the car could even be stolen. Many nations have Government or private organisations that will supply for a fee accurate and complete vehicle ownership data, based on the car's licence plate number and/or VIN. These organisations can often also provide information related to the car's accident history such as: has the car previously been declared 'written-off' by an insurance company after an accident. In the UK the following organisations can supply vehicle data:

DVLA   0844 453 0118
HPI   0113 222 2010
AA   0800 056 8040
RAC   0330 159 0364

Unleaded fuel
The entire 986 series model range was designed to run on unleaded fuel only.

Insurance
Check with your existing insurer before setting out; your current policy, or that of the vendor, may not cover you to drive the car if you do purchase it. Do not drive uninsured cars and, if in doubt, always ask.

How can you pay?
A cheque (check) will take several days to clear and the seller may prefer to sell to a cash buyer. However, a banker's draft (a cheque issued by a bank) is as good as cash, but safer, so contact your own bank and become familiar with the formalities that are necessary to obtain one.

Buying at auction?
If the intention is to buy at auction see chapter 10 for further advice.

Professional vehicle check (mechanical examination)
There are often marque/model specialists who will undertake professional examination of a vehicle on your behalf. Owners' clubs will be able to put you in touch with specialists and Porsche dealerships offer similar services.

6 Inspection equipment
– these items will really help

Before you rush out the door, gather together a few items that will help as you complete a more thorough inspection.

This book
Reading glasses (if you need them for close work)
Magnet (not powerful, a fridge magnet is ideal)
Torch (flashlight)
Probe (a small screwdriver works very well)
Overalls
Mirror on a stick
Digital camera
A companion

This book is designed to be your guide at every step, so take it along and use the check boxes to help you assess each area of the car you're interested in. Don't be afraid to let the seller see you using it.

Take your reading glasses if you need them to read documents and make close-up inspections. The author has to take his off for close-up work, so carry a glasses case if you have to do the same.

A magnet will help you check if the car is full of filler, or has fibreglass or carbon-fibre panels. Ask the seller's permission before using a magnet: some may prefer you to use a paint depth meter. If permission is granted use the magnet to sample bodywork areas all around the car, but be careful not to damage the paintwork.

A torch with fresh batteries will be useful for peering into the front spoiler to check radiator condition, but remember the 986 Boxster models have many panels covering up entire areas, including the engine which is nicely hidden away.

A small screwdriver can be used – with care – as a probe, particularly in the wheelarches and on the underside. However, 986 Boxster models suffering from structural corrosion are extremely rare, so be careful what you start probing and always ask the seller's permission before taking metal implements anywhere near the paintwork.

Be prepared to get dirty. Take along a pair of overalls, if you have them.

Fixing a mirror at an angle on the end of a stick may seem odd, but you'll probably need it to check the condition of the underside of the car. It will also help you to peer into some of the important crevices. You can also use it, together with the torch, along the underside of the sills and on the floor: remember that a completely original 986 Boxster is panelled the entire length of its underside.

A digital camera is an essential piece of inspection equipment. If you don't have one, use your mobile phone. Take lots of pictures of all parts of the car whether or not they cause you concern. When you get home study them and, if in doubt, seek an expert's opinion. Sometimes photographs viewed in the quiet of your own home will reveal things you missed in the heat of the moment.

Have a friend or knowledgeable enthusiast accompany you: a second opinion is always valuable, and another person provides a level of personal security.

7 Fifteen minute evaluation
– walk away or stay?

Exterior

Ensuring the 986 Boxster is parked on level ground, start the exterior inspection by looking for obvious signs of body damage and accident repairs.

Walk around the car randomly, but carefully, placing the magnet onto areas of the bodywork. If it sticks move on, if it not, find out why.

Corrosion (rust) damage is easy to spot as the paint will be bubbled and/or cracked. Randomly measure the body panel gaps, around the front and rear luggage compartment lids and the doors. If the gaps are even it usually means the body is straight. Major inconsistencies in gaps indicate the car has been repaired after a major accident.

Look for obvious signs of repainting such as different shades and overspray.

Porsche paintwork is of the highest quality. The best place to look for overspray is in hard-to-get-at places, such as forward of the doors or under the wheel wells. A poor repaint is an immediate reason to walk away. A good quality repaint should not deter you from purchasing, but allow renegotiation of the price – downwards! Inspect for minor front or rear end collisions by checking bumper mouldings for cracks and splits in the plastic.

Check the panel gaps for consistency.
(Courtesy Bob Schoenherr)

Standard 986 Boxster rear spoiler (wing) extended.
(Courtesy Porsche AG archive)

Check around the combined headlight and indicator assemblies for stone chip damage and cracked lenses. With the aid of your torch and through the front spoiler check the condition of the front mounted radiators. The number of radiators installed is model dependent. The Boxster model range has two radiators (left and right). The Boxster S has three with the addition of a centre radiator as part of Option M008. One issue related to Porsche AG's excellent aerodynamic design is that as it draws cooling air through the radiators it also acts as a powerful vacuum cleaner, sucking up anything it can from the road surface. Ensure the radiators have been cleared of all debris. Organic materials decay and can cause all kinds of corrosion issues as the car ages.

Check the condition of the rear lights' lens assemblies.

Check all door and window seals.

Ensure the seller extends the rear spoiler (wing) fully open and inspect for evidence of damage, rubbing and corrosion. Once completed ask the seller to retract the rear spoiler to its full down position whilst you watch to see if everything runs smoothly.

Whilst inspecting the exterior check the brake discs (rotors), callipers and pads. Pad friction material thickness must be greater than 2mm (0.08in), and the discs must not be damaged. Check for evidence of brake fluid leakage over any components in the wheel wells, including at the rear of each wheel.

Check the condition of suspension components in the wheel wells.

Ask the seller to operate the powered roof (fully open to fully closed), and then thoroughly inspect the fabric as it's very expensive to replace. Ensure the roof stowage cover also opens and closes smoothly. Check sealing, water drains and the condition of the plastic rear window (glass from model year 2003), as well as condition and alignment of the frame with the roof open and closed. Ask the seller if there have been any roof repairs carried out. There is an optional hardtop available for the Boxster. If the sale includes such a roof assembly, inspect for matching colour, overall condition, and that all fittings are in good order.

When carrying out an exterior inspection always check the ground under the car for evidence of fluid leaks: oil, coolant, transmission oil, water and/or hydraulic fluid.

Interior

Inspect all interior fittings and assemblies, including a full inspection of each seat for condition, ensuring none of the main or trim materials are cracked, torn, faded or missing. A cracked dashboard is extremely expensive to repair. Lower the rear seat backs and check behind. Inspect the instruments for damage or fading. Ensure the internal lighting system works.

Check all electric seat functions. If one set of controls is not working, it's possible that those functions were never installed by the factory (check the options list). If seat heating is installed, check this as well. These items are often overlooked and are expensive to repair. Ask the seller if there have been any problems with the airbags. Some owners disconnect the passenger airbag so children can occupy the passenger seat. If disabled ensure it's clearly labelled as such. Check that all the combined interior light and switch assemblies operate correctly, and inspect the light assemblies (which vary in location and design between models).

Check for moisture in the carpets and, if possible, check the condition of the control units installed under both seats.

Run the electric windows down and back up to see if there's any moisture trapped in the door. Empty the contents of each door pocket and check for moisture. A good tip is to wipe the inside of each pocket with a tissue (Kleenex) and see if it picks up anything. Empty the contents of the glovebox (if installed) and check for evidence of moisture, damage to switches and cables; does the light come on? Check if there's an owner's manual somewhere in the car.

Compartments and mechanicals

Open both the front and rear luggage compartment lids. Ensure the luggage compartment lid gas struts hold up the lids. Inspect any visible seals which run around the body in the vicinity of the lids for condition, and check for any evidence of moisture. The 986 Boxster luggage compartments are fully panelled, and inspecting

Rear luggage
compartment.
(Courtesy Russ Standage)

Front and rear luggage
compartment lid
release levers.
(Courtesy Bob Schoenherr)

Front luggage
compartment.
(Courtesy Bob Schoenherr)

the items beneath requires the co-operation of the seller in order to gain access. There are easy items to inspect in the front luggage compartment, such as the battery. Remove the plastic battery cover in the centre rear of the compartment and inspect the battery for condition and any evidence of acid spill and/or corrosion. Check the compartment's panelled areas for moisture damage and staining. If everything is clean, what lies beneath is probably in good condition. All 986 Boxster models are fitted with a collapsible spare tyre assembly installed in the front luggage compartment. Remove its cover and inspect. Ensure the air-compressor and associated accessories are present.

Beginning the process of gaining access to the top of the engine. (Courtesy Bob Schoenherr)

Open up the tool kit and check that all tools are present, are original Porsche items and are not damaged or rusty. Check the wheel jack and brace for operation and condition.

Top engine compartment lid finally exposed. (Courtesy Bob Schoenherr)

Top of the engine exposed for a mandatory inspection. (Courtesy Bob Schoenherr)

Access to part of the engine is from the passenger compartment. (Courtesy Bob Schoenherr)

Accessing the Boxster's engine requires the assistance of the seller. There are two engine compartment lids/panels that need to be accessed. To get to the top engine compartment cover (lid) the roof must be placed in a partially raised position, with the front of the roof stopped approximately 40cm away from the windscreen (windshield). Remove the ignition key to ensure the roof cannot move from this position. Follow the rear roof section disconnecting and restraining procedures in the owner's manual or get the seller to do it. Then follow the manual's procedures to gain access to the engine compartment lid and, finally, remove the top engine compartment lid itself. With access to the top of the engine now available carry out a basic inspection of the engine and its components, looking for obvious signs of oil, coolant and power-steering fluid leakage. Access to the engine-driven belt and some accessories is through a separate panel which itself is accessed from the inside rear section of the passenger compartment.

All 986 Boxster models, for all markets, from model year 1997 are fitted with a secondary air injection (SAI) system. Also check for obvious engine modifications (tuning companies often leave some form of advertising material behind). If a part doesn't have a Porsche part number it's usually not original. If in doubt, question the seller.

Is it genuine and legal?
Ask the seller for all documentation related to the car, including owner's manual, service record book, emission inspection reports, any import documentation, roadworthiness inspection certificates and all repair receipts.

Check the service record book: is it the original or a replacement (duplicate)? A duplicate record book will have 'duplicate' stamped on each page.

Under the luggage compartment lid, at the front near the locking latch, is a white label and the information it contains is very important to check the authenticity of the car. The most important is the Vehicle identification number (VIN): 17 digits of which the 10th digit indicates the model year. It also tells you the type (or model) code, engine type, engine code, transmission type, paint code, interior colour combination code, country code and the options installed. If this label is missing ask the seller why? A computer generated printed copy of this label can only be found in an original service record book. If the seller cannot answer why the label(s) are missing, and/or cannot provide original documentation walk away.

The VIN on the label must match the VIN found at numerous locations in the car, such as behind the windscreen (windshield), and in the top rear right (as viewed from driver's seat) of the luggage compartment (viewed through a peephole), and these VINs must also match national registration and insurance documentation. The Porsche 986 Boxster and Boxster S models were either manufactured in Stuttgart Germany by Porsche AG or in Uusikaupunki Finland by Valmet. This means the 11th digit of the VIN will be 'S' for 986s manufactured in Germany and 'U' for those manufactured in Finland.

Vehicle identification label on the underside of the front luggage compartment lid. It's critically important that what's printed on this label matches what it's attached to. (Courtesy Bob Schoenherr)

A proper authenticity check also includes physically inspecting the engine ID plate, looking for its type and date of manufacture codes, and ensuring that these numbers match the type and codes on the identification label. Again, the full engine serial number must match all registration documentation. An important authenticity check is to confirm the 986 Boxster's paint code. Match the code on the identification label with the label found on the left side of the luggage compartment under the carpeted panelling.

Questions to ask the seller

There are some things that only the most experienced 986 Boxster expert is going to find during a 15 minute inspection. For the first-time buyer it's much better to go armed with the important questions:
• Was this 986 Boxster originally built for the market (country) it's being sold in?
• Has this car been used for track days, including driver education events, or been used in any form of motor sport?
• Is the mileage genuine?
• Is the car a weekend warrior, or was it used as a daily driver?
• Was it regularly driven in heavy traffic?
• Has the car been involved in an accident?
• Has the engine and/or transmission been repaired or modified?
• Are there any known problems with any of the car's electrical or electronic systems?
    You'll need to decide whether or not you're being told the truth: if you purchase a 986 Boxster with problems, returning it to good health can be extremely frustrating.

Restoration of a basket case

There are very few 986 Boxsters basket cases around, if any (the author has not seen any), and those that are will usually be accident wrecks. It's not worth purchasing a wreck as restoration is not an economic option for the Boxster range, unless the purchase price is very low ... and you are a masochist.

8 Key points
– where to look for problems

Paying particular attention to, and understanding, what you are looking at!

Get up-close and personal to check thoroughly. (Courtesy Russ Standage)

Left-hand radiators can be seen through the front spoiler ... (Courtesy Bob Schoenherr)

... as can the right-hand.
(Courtesy Bob Schoenherr)

Headlight lenses require careful and close inspection.
(Courtesy Bob Schoenherr)

You should also get up-close and personal with the rear light lenses. (Courtesy Mac Cranford owner and D Randy Riggs photographer)

Are the wheels Porsche approved? Also inspect what's behind the wheel spokes. (Courtesy Mac Cranford owner & D Randy Riggs photographer)

The data on the label on the underside of the luggage compartment is very important. (Courtesy Bob Schoenherr)

The battery compartment is located in the front luggage compartment. (Courtesy Bob Schoenherr)

Part of the 986 Boxster 2.5-litre engine accessed through the top cover. (Courtesy Bob Schoenherr)

Belts and accessories of the 986 Boxster 2.5-litre engine are accessed through a panel (here sitting on armrest) at the rear of the passenger compartment. (Courtesy Bob Schoenherr)

9 Serious evaluation
– 60 minutes for years of enjoyment

Circle Excellent (4), Good (3), Average (2) or Poor (1) boxes for each check and add up points at the end of the inspection procedure. Any evaluation check must be realistic. Sole responsibility lies with the buyer to be vigilant and not cut corners over the next 60 minutes. Take it seriously, get it right, and you will be able to make an informed decision on whether to purchase this particular car, or not, and you keep your family relationships intact! Get it wrong and it could be your worst nightmare come true ...

How does it look just sitting there?

The 986 Boxster is a thoroughbred sports car manufactured for high performance motoring. It is not a toy and, if it's not set up properly, it will bite its owner. Before starting any evaluation ensure the 986 Boxster is parked on level ground. Does it sit level? Look at it from all angles. Is it clean inside and out? Does it look smart or a little tired? Does it smell of fast food? Does it look original? What's your first impression? This first rating is based on first impressions.

First impressions count. (Courtesy Mac Cranford owner and D Randy Riggs photographer)

Exterior and interior colour combination

Everybody thinks at some time about the resale value of their cars. One huge value killer can be the exterior and interior colour combination. Men can be very practical on this subject and say: "I could get used to it" or "I can learn to live with it." Rating is for an honest opinion from *all* involved.

Exterior paint

When inspecting a car's paintwork/ bodywork remember that it is always easier to repair/ replace mechanical items than to do work of any type on the car's bodywork. The 986 Boxster is difficult to repair properly, especially structurally, and the Porsche workshop manual repair schemes are complicated requiring specialist equipment. In reality there are two types of repairs that are carried out: (1) repair immediately at minimum cost and pass the problem to a new owner;

What about the exterior and interior colour combination? Does it work for you? (Courtesy Russ Standage)

(2) keep the car after a thorough, high-quality repair (such permanent repairs are possible, but only if carried out by an experienced professional who won't cut corners). This is why an inspection and assessment of the paintwork is so critical: how it's done is covered in chapter 7, but if there are any doubts take as much time as you like before making an assessment decision. Rust is not a major issue in the 986 Boxster, but poor accident damage repairs have been identified within

Seriously, you need to get up-close and personal to inspect the paintwork properly.
(Courtesy Bob Schoenherr)

the Boxster community, and rust could develop in the repaired areas. Rating is for condition.

Body panel condition (including door bases)

Battle damage from debris on the road is a fact of life. A normal unmodified 986 Boxster sits significantly lower than standard road cars and is always in the firing line. If the car is completely clean without any evidence of stone chips it indicates that it hasn't been driven much or it's recently been repaired and/or completely repainted.

Body panel damage

Small dents and scrapes have to be assessed during the inspection. Scratches around the door locks and handles are quite normal, but the question for the buyer is always: can the visible damage be repaired using the latest minor dent removal technologies, or is a more serious and costly repair required?

Panel gaps

Walk around the car with a ruler and measure the gaps between all moving panels and surrounding metalwork, which all should all be even. Don't forget to compare one side of the car with the

Inspect the side air vents for condition, and ensure they're not blocked.
(Courtesy Bob Schoenherr)

Boxster cutaway diagram helps with locating items.
(Courtesy Porsche AG archive)

It's probably a good idea to remove all items in the front luggage compartment before inspecting it. (Courtesy Porsche AG archive)

other. Rating is for irregularities in gap measurements and visible damage, no matter how small or seemingly insignificant.

Seals ④ ③ ② ①

Check the condition of all visible rubber seals, especially those around the front windscreen (windshield), and rear window (plastic or glass from model year 2003) installed in the roadster rag top. Don't forget to inspect all hardtop seals and rear window installation if it's part of the purchase package. Check the rubber seals around the door frames, front and rear luggage compartment lids, and, if accessible, the internal engine compartment lids/covers. Seal damage provides an entry path for water, which will cause problems later in the Boxster's life. Rating is for condition and replacement cost if any seals are damaged.

Radiators & coolant colour ④ ③ ② ①

Radiator condition can only be assessed by a visual inspection of what can be seen through the front spoiler using a torch. If the 986 Boxster is fitted with

The brake fluid reservoir is located in the front luggage compartment. (Courtesy Bob Schoenherr)

Radiators are well protected behind the front spoiler, but access is difficult. (Courtesy Porsche AG archive)

Better view of a coolant radiator assembly. (Courtesy Porsche AG archive)

Check the coolant colour here.
(Courtesy Russ Standage)

air-conditioning the condenser-mixer assemblies are actually mounted in front of the left and right side radiators, so it's the condenser-mixers that are really being inspected. The general rule is that if the mixers are in good condition the actual coolant radiators behind them should also be in good condition. If you wish full access to the radiators for a detailed inspection the front section underside panel and bumper moulding have to be removed. The number of coolant radiators installed is Boxster model dependent. The 2.5- and 2.7-litre-powered models have two coolant radiators, left and right. The 3.2-litre powered Boxster S and Boxster S 550 Spyder models have three: left, centre and right. It's not possible to visually inspect all the individual components in the engine coolant system. However, a check of the coolant colour in the overflow/filling container in the rear luggage compartment will provide an excellent overview of system condition. Original coolant colour will be

dependent on local products used, but if the coolant has mixed with any other fluid in the engine, transmission or via one of the heat exchangers it will be muddy brown. If the current owner has not used the proper coolant/anti-freeze mixture, and used water instead, the coolant will also be muddy brown. Contaminated coolant is a reason to stop the inspection and walk away. Rating is for condenser-mixer/radiator assembly condition and coolant colour.

Correct operation of all lights must be ascertained. (Courtesy Bob Schoenherr)

Lights
Check the condition and operation of all installed lighting systems front and rear, including headlights, rear lights, indicators (turn signals) front, rear and side, brake, reverse and foglights. Rating is for overall condition and correct operation.

Wipers
Check condition and operation of the front wiper arm assemblies, including the wiper blades. Rating is for condition and operation (don't forget to wet the glass first).

Washers
Check condition of the windscreen (windshield) and

Headlight washer nozzles, if installed, must also be inspected. (Courtesy Mac Cranford owner and D Randy Riggs photographer)

headlight (if installed) washer nozzles and operate the system. Rating is for washer nozzle condition and spray operation.

Roadster rag top (soft top) ④ ③ ② ①

All 986 Boxsters are of the roadster body style and were delivered as standard with an electric-powered rag top roof. A thorough inspection and functional check of the entire rag top system is highly recommended. Pre-model year 2003 Boxsters were all fitted with plastic rear windows that are notoriously hard to repair; from model year 2003 all Boxsters were fitted with glass rear windows, and these are even harder to repair. Roadster fabric roof systems often creak, groan and moan, but the sound of fabric ripping can be very annoying as well as being expensive to repair. Carry out an inspection with the roof fully up, in mid position and fully down and stowed. Rating is for rag top fabric, frame, window and seal condition and a full operational check.

Roadster hardtop ④ ③ ② ①

An optional lightweight Porsche-manufactured hardtop was available for all 986 Boxster models. If a hardtop is included as part of the purchase, ensure it's painted in the same colour as the car's exterior. It should also be accompanied with specific Boxster installation accessories, so ensure these are also included. Refer to the owner's manual for full details. Rating is for roof and accessories condition.

Ask the seller to operate the roof. (Courtesy Porsche AG archive)

What lies beneath? Every component in the Roadster roof system must be inspected. (Courtesy Russ Standage)

Always inspect the roof interior condition and mechanism: roof release not pressed ... (Courtesy Russ Standage)

... roof release pressed. (Courtesy Russ Standage)

Check the roadster roof condition inside and out in various positions like this ... (Courtesy Russ Standage)

... and this ... (Courtesy Russ Standage)

... and this. (Courtesy Russ Standage)

Don't forget the hardtop if it's included in the sale. (Courtesy Porsche AG archive)

Inspect the wind deflector assembly. (Courtesy Bob Schoenherr)

Windscreen (windshield) [4] [3] [2] [1]

Before carrying out a vehicle inspection find out what national rules apply to the windscreen (windshield) regarding acceptable damage. Is a single chip or crack sufficient to fail a roadworthiness inspection? Rating is for windscreen condition and how it impacts roadworthiness.

Door glass

Operate the powered door windows. Ensure they

Check the windscreen (windshield) for chips, cracks, and the VIN. (Author collection)

What rating should the condition of this wheel be? Is it approved for the 986 Boxster? Yes! (Courtesy Russ Standage)

move up and down freely without making any weird and wonderful sounds. Also check to see if any moisture is present on the glass after they have been run down and back up again. Check also that the windows seal correctly into the rag top when it's fully up and locked. Rating is for condition, correct relative noiseless operation and detected moisture.

Wheels   4️⃣   3️⃣   2️⃣   1️⃣

Check the wheels are correct for the model being inspected by comparing what's physically installed with the owner's manual. Incorrect wheels can cause serious problems including wheel rub and unsafe handling. This inspection relates to safety as well as roadworthiness. If there's any doubt ask the seller for additional paperwork on the wheels. The condition of each wheel is critically important as corrosion can lead

Inspect behind the wheels' spokes. (Courtesy Bob Schoenherr)

to fatigue cracking and structural failure. Genuine Porsche factory wheels are clear coated and if this coating is peeling it will be costly to get it repaired. Inspect for impact damage around the rim. Look at the relationship between the wheels and the wheel arch. Rating is for wheel originality and condition.

Wheel well linings   4️⃣   3️⃣   2️⃣   1️⃣

Ensure all are fitted. Check condition of the plastic and mounting screws. Rating is for condition.

Wheel bearings and halfshafts   4️⃣   3️⃣   2️⃣   1️⃣

Porsche wheel bearings are almost bullet proof and rarely fail. To check the wheel bearing remove the wheel centre cap and using a torch inspect for evidence of metal filings and overheating. A failed wheel bearing

Only a test drive is going to reveal wheel bearing issues. (Courtesy Porsche AG archive)

will get very hot; will blue the cotter pin and burn the lubricating grease within the bearing, and will deposit soot around the wheel bearing housing. If metal debris or evidence of overheating is discovered, jack the affected wheel off the ground and rotate it. If grinding scraping noises are heard it's likely either the wheel bearing and/or the halfshaft CV joint has failed. However, the test drive will reveal any rotating part with failed bearing surfaces because it will scream like a Banshee. Locating the source of the noise, however, will require a thorough inspection. Rating is for condition of the wheel bearing and if a further more detailed inspection is warranted.

Tyre condition, suitability and wheel alignment ④ ③ ② ①

See chapter 17 for Porsche-approved tyres for the 986 Boxster. (Courtesy Porsche AG archive)

Who owns a thoroughbred sports car capable of high speeds and installs cheap tyres or mixes and matches tyre brands from side-to-side and front-to-rear in order to save money? Only a fool. The four black round bits of rubber wrapped around the wheels are the only things safely connecting the Boxster to the road. Why spend a huge amount of money purchasing a precision high performance sports car and then put everyone at risk by installing cheap useless tyres? A set of approved and tested tyres for the car not only gives it the ability to perform at its maximum in the handling department, but also allows the maximum transfer of power to the road and ensures the braking system provides maximum stopping power at all times.

The 986 Boxster model range is designed to be driven on approved summer tyres in summer and the approved and/or tested winter tyres in winter: it was not designed to be driven fitted with all-season el-cheapo jack-of-all trade tyres. Don't drive a Boxster on summer tyres when the road temperature drops below 7°C (45°F), switch to winter tyres. Why? Winter tyres are made from a softer compound, heat up more quickly, and don't go hard. To give just one example: If the road is wet and is at a temperature of 7°C (45°F) the summer tyres will require 38% more braking distance to stop from 80kph (50mph) to a full stop as compared to the winter tyres.

Uneven tyre wear is an indicator of wheel alignment issues. (Author collection)

Check tyres for same brand, same tread pattern, correct size front and rear for the installed wheels and in accordance with the owner's manual (see the table in chapter 17 which contains an up-to-date list of all tyres approved and tested by Porsche for the 986 series). Look at the wear across each tyre. Is it even? Is there more on the outside than inside, or vice versa? Bad wheel alignment will causes tyres to wear unevenly. Rating is for tyre condition (blisters and cracks), uneven wear, age (more than six years old), suitability and cost of a wheel alignment if required.

Steering system

All 986 Boxster models are fitted with powered (boosted) rack and pinion steering. The power steering system requires the engine to be running and any grinding and air cavitations noises from the engine mounted power steering pump will be obvious. With the engine running turn the steering wheel full left and then full right, listening for any unusual sounds.

Check under the middle and front of the car for any fluid leakage, which may not be immediately obvious, so slide some butcher's paper (described later under oil leaks) under the front and under right side of the engine then come back later to check. Rating is for system component inspection and condition, static test with engine running and any detected fluid leaks.

Standard 2.5-litre 986 Boxster 4-piston brake calliper. (Courtesy Bob Schoenherr)

Brake callipers and pads

A basic brake calliper inspection can be carried out by looking through the wheels, but it's better to have the front wheels turned full left and then full right to allow better access to the callipers and to be able to view the brake pads. Inspect the brake pads: each should have friction material more than 2mm thick. Pads must be changed at 2mm to ensure the pad wear warning detectors are not activated because, if they are, they have to be replaced as well. Rating is for calliper condition as well as brake pad thickness.

Standard 2.5-litre 986 Boxster calliper, but with aftermarket brake disc (rotor). (Courtesy Bob Schoenherr)

986 Boxster S with red-painted front and rear brake callipers. (Courtesy Mac Cranford owner and D Randy Riggs photographer)

Check the brake pad friction material thickness. (Courtesy Bob Schoenherr)

Brake discs (rotors)

All 986 Boxster models were delivered with steel perforated and ventilated front and rear brake discs (rotors). Check each brake disc for wear looking for cracks between the holes, blocked holes and grooves worn into the disc. Consideration has to be given to overall brake disc thickness which during such an evaluation is hard to check. Look at each disc carefully. Is there a lip or edge cut around the outer circumference? Such a lip indicates that the brake pads have worn away both faces of the brake disc and that, at the next service, all discs will have to be replaced. Rating is for brake disc condition and wear.

Hand (emergency/parking) brake ④ ③ ② ①

The hand (emergency/parking) brake must be tested to ensure it holds the car stationary under all circumstances. Rating is for brake holding ability.

Rear spoiler (wing) ④ ③ ② ①

Standard 986 Boxsters were delivered with a vertical moving, electro-mechanical extend and retract rear spoiler (wing) system, installed in the body directly behind the rear luggage compartment lid. Porsche Exclusive offered an optional fixed rear spoiler (wing) as part of an aerokit, and at least one design is fitted with brake lights. If the standard rear spoiler (wing) is installed, ask the seller to extend it. Whilst the mechanism is running ensure it does not bind or jam. Once it's fully extended check the condition of all visible parts. Ask the seller to retract it, ensuring it retracts correctly, smoothly, and stows evenly. Rating

Standard rear spoiler (wing) installed at rear of luggage compartment lid. (Courtesy Porsche AG archive)

Standard rear spoiler (wing) extended. (Courtesy Porsche AG archive)

Optional Boxster S fixed rear spoiler
(wing) from Porsche Exclusive.
(Courtesy Porsche AG archive)

is for rear spoiler (wing) condition
and electro-mechanical operation, if
applicable.

Engine
inspection

In every model in the 986 Boxster
range the engine is the most difficult
component to gain access to, as
explained in chapter 7. The top of
the engine can only be accessed by
carrying out a complicated exercise
starting by positioning the rag top
roof in a specific position and then
following all the procedures laid down
in the owner's manual. The engine-
driven belts and some engine-driven
accessories can only be accessed by
gaining access to, and then removing,
the engine compartment cover
located in the rear of the passenger
compartment. The underside of the
engine can only be accessed from
underneath. When inspecting the
engine ensure you are aware of the
actual model of Boxster and what
engine size should be installed. There
are a few Boxsters around with
tuned 911 engines installed. The 986
Boxster only has one belt driving all
engine accessories, so its condition
is very important. Corrosion on the
engine and associated components is
quite common if the 986 Boxster has
been driven in winter. Check for any
visible forms of engine modifications.
If anything causes alarm, ask the
seller about it. Rating is for condition
of all visible components, component
originality, all visible metal work and
engine bay cleanliness.

Optional Boxster fixed rear spoiler (wing)
design from Porsche Exclusive.
(Courtesy Porsche AG archive)

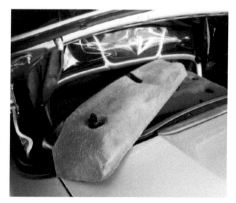

Accessing the 986 Boxster's engine is
quite a drawn-out process.
(Courtesy Bob Schoenherr)

Another panel has to be opened to get to the engine-driven belt and engine-driven accessories. (Courtesy Bob Schoenherr)

It's pretty tight in there. Notice the K&N air filter label. (Courtesy Bob Schoenherr)

Fuel cap cover and luggage compartments 4 3 2 1

Open the fuel filler cap and check for correct labelling. (Courtesy Bob Schoenherr)

The fuel cap cover in the 986 Boxster series is located on the right side wing (fender/guard), and can be opened by hand anytime the doors are unlocked. Open and check the condition of the fuel cap and ensure the required labels are installed on the cover underside. These labels vary with national requirements. Check the fuel cap cover is locked when the doors are locked.

The luggage compartment's lids are released using levers (model years 1997 to 2000) or electrical switches installed in the driver's side door sill (from model year 2001). Start inspection of the front luggage compartment lid. Lift it to its full open position and ensure the gas struts hold it open. Major fixed components in the front luggage compartment such as the fuel tank are not easily accessed. The battery cover can be removed and the battery and surrounds inspected. The spare collapsible wheel and tyre assembly along with the tool kit is also accessible and can be easily inspected. If the seller agrees, a panel can be removed (tools required) to expose the paint code label on the lower left side, but this should only be done if there is any doubt about the exterior colour being original. Ensure the wheel jack and associated safety accessories, as

Collapsible spare wheel and tyre assembly and tools. (Courtesy Bob Schoenherr)

Front luggage compartment. (Courtesy Bob Schoenherr)

required by local law, are installed. Open the tool kit and check all the tools are accounted for and in good condition. Sustained water ingress will cause the tools to rust. Move to the rear luggage compartment and ensure the gas struts hold up its lid. Inspect the carpet for condition and any evidence of contamination. Coolant and oil systems are checked via access points in the rear luggage compartment. Rating is for condition of all components that can be inspected, luggage compartment condition and the presence and condition of all required accessories, tools and emergency equipment.

Battery is easily accessed in the front luggage compartment. (Courtesy Bob Schoenherr)

Battery charging rate

With the engine running at idle, connect a digital multi-meter across the battery terminals and the voltage shown on the display must be between 13.8 and 14.2 volts DC. To check battery condition, turn off the engine and measure the voltage between the terminals again and it should be between 12.4 and 12.6 volts DC.

Rating is based on voltage measurements in both tests. For example: 13.8 volts DC and 12.6 volts DC = 4. More than 14.2 volts DC and less than 12.4 volts DC = 1.

Tow hook

The tow hook can be installed into a threaded section of the body structure accessed through the front or rear bumper moulding, the holes of which are covered with small, easily removed plastic covers. A quick check to ensure the unibody (combined chassis and body structure) is straight is to insert the tow hook. If the tow hook starts to resist and twists at an angle or cannot even be inserted straight this is a definite sign of an accident damaged and bent unibody. Rating is a pass with deductions for tow hook, bumper bar hole and cover condition. Walk away if the car fails this test.

Interior water ingress check

Open the doors and check along the bottom of each one for water. Run the electric door windows down and up to see if the window picks up any moisture. Open each door storage compartment checking for obvious signs of dampness or water damaged contents. Dab a Kleenex tissue around any suspect areas inside the car, including the carpets, to see if it picks up moisture. Rating is for detected moisture.

Interior

The interior inspection is all about originality of installed seats, rollover bar, seatbelts dashboard, carpet, mats and trim. Inspect for rips,

Many interior options were offered by Porsche Exclusive. (Courtesy Porsche AG archive)

tears, staining, mould, repairs and fraying seatbelts. Is the seatbelt lower stitched loop still intact? (if it's been in an accident the loop will have broken on impact), check the operation of seatbelt inertia reels front and rear, and for any other damage. Check that all the interior lights function when the doors are opened (on) and closed (off). Check all electrical and mechanical functions of the driver and passenger seats in accordance with the owner's manual. Check condition and operation of the wind deflector. Check condition of the rollover bar and its associated linings. Ensure the central locking system functions correctly by using the door key (driver's side only), and by using the internal locking button. Check that when the doors are locked the alarm system indicator light in the dash is flashing at a rate of once per second once the alarm system has finished its self-test program. Rating is for overall condition, operation of electrical and mechanical seat functions, central locking, alarm system indication, and interior lighting operation.

Always inspect the seatbacks and pockets for damage. (Courtesy Bob Schoenherr)

Steering wheel, horn & steering column control stalks

Inspect the airbag steering wheel for condition. Check horn operation. Check all steering column stalk functions. Rating is for steering wheel condition, horn operation, and condition and operation of each stalk lever.

Instrument cluster

The 986 Boxster series was offered with numerous instrument dial and bezel colours in various materials, including aluminium, carbon fibre, and wood. Check the option package for the car before concluding anything is not original. Check that each instrument's internal lighting is functioning correctly when the headlights are turned on, and check the light system dimming – the operation of which depends on installed options (see the owner's manual). Rating is for instrument condition and correct internal lighting operation.

986 Boxster Tiptronic steering wheel. (Courtesy Porsche AG archive)

Warning and advisory lights

Consult the owner's manual warning light system

Instrument warning and advisory lights illuminated. (Courtesy Porsche AG archive)

pages as it's important to know what warning lights are fitted to a specific model and where everything is installed, including switches. Engage the hand (parking/emergency) brake and turn on the ignition, but do not start the engine. The warning system electronics will illuminate and then test all warning and advisory lights. Ensure all warning lights that should be are illuminated are. If there are any doubts read the owner's manual again or ask the seller. Rating is for condition of warning and advisory lights including symbols and correct operation.

The next stage is put the 986 Boxster onto a lifter or over a pit and carry out some basic inspections from underneath.

Lift the Boxster and inspect underneath. (Courtesy Bob Schoenherr)

View from underneath with underside panels in place. (Courtesy Bob Schoenherr)

It's better to inspect the suspension from underneath. (Courtesy Bob Schoenherr)

Underside panels 4 3 2 1

Every road legal 986 Boxster was fitted with three separate underside panels: front, centre and rear. Check all are present, and look closely for any evidence of scrap marks or impact damage. Never purchase a 986 Boxster without its underside panels. Rating is for condition of panels and sealing.

Oil filter. (Courtesy Bob Schoenherr)

Suspension 4 3 2 1

A visual inspection of the Boxster wheel wells from underneath should reveal any suspension issues. Check for any aftermarket modifications to the suspension. If in doubt ask the seller. Rating is for suspension condition and detected aftermarket modifications.

Exhaust system

4 3 2 1

Because the 986 Boxster is not fitted with a full rear cover much of the exhaust system can be easily inspected. Ask the seller if any exhaust modifications have been carried out. Rating is for exhaust system originality and condition.

The entire exhaust system can be inspected from underneath. (Courtesy Autofarm (1973) Ltd)

Catalytic converter and oxygen sensor condition is very important. (Courtesy Bob Schoenherr)

Oil leaks

4 3 2 1

One of the best oil leak checks that can be carried out is done after the test drive. Park the 986 Boxster on level ground and slide some butcher's paper under the engine, go away come back after thirty to sixty minutes. Pull out the paper and check how much oil has dripped on the paper. Rating is for any detected oil leaks during the static inspection and/or after the test drive.

Coolant leaks

4 3 2 1

Check the ground under the front spoiler, around each front wheel and underneath the rear of the car for any for any evidence of radiator coolant leakage. Rating is for detected leaks.

Transmission fluid and water leaks

4 3 2 1

Evidence of transmission fluid leaks and water leaks from the installed washer system can usually be detected in the vent holes of the underside panels. Rating is for detected leaks.

Test drive

4 3 2 1

This is mandatory. During the test drive every system must be tested including the air conditioning, heating, sound, etc. Everything with a button must be switched on and tested. The test drive rating must reflect the correct function of every system, handling, braking efficiency, acceleration and gear changing and the intensity of the smile on your face.

A test drive is mandatory, as is the smile you'll wear. (Author collection)

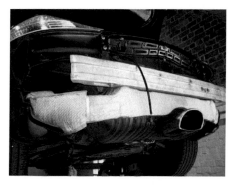

Don't play hard ball as things can get messy. (Courtesy Autofarm (1973) Ltd)

Light and rose-tinted glasses can cover a multitude of sins, but this puppy is a perfect example: top 1%. (Courtesy Mac Cranford owner and D Randy Riggs photographer)

Playing hardball

Some buyers demand engine leak down and compression checks be carried out requiring invasive surgery, many sellers naturally refuse. Less invasive methods are available such as carrying out an exhaust gas analysis in conjunction with a Porsche PS-2 tester or later equivalent plugged into the car's diagnostic port. A knowledgeable diagnostic equipment operator can quickly identify any problems and the exhaust gas analysis will reveal engine and/or exhaust system internal problems. Rating is for passing one or both tests, full points to null points (and walk away).

Evaluation procedure
Add up the points scored!

150 to 160 points = excellent to almost concours class, hope it doesn't break.
140 to 149 points = good to very good, but it's going to cost to keep it this way.
120 to 139 points = average to good, but where were the problems found?
110 to 119 points = below average to average and careful consideration required.
100 to 109 points = border line money pit.
80 to 99 points = beware it's going to cost a lot of money, what's the purchase price?
79 points or less = run away unless you want to turn a big fortune into a small one.

If any Porsche 986 Boxster scores less than 100 from such a detailed inspection the buyer needs to carefully consider their purchasing position because it's definitely going to be a money pit. Restoration of such a complicated piece of machinery to full roadworthiness is a labour of love as the money sunk into it cannot be recovered.

10 Auctions
– sold! Another way to buy your dream

Auction pros & cons
Pros: Prices will usually be lower than those of dealers or private sellers and you might grab a real bargain on the day. Auctioneers have usually established clear title with the seller. At the venue you can usually examine documentation relating to the vehicle. Cons: You have to rely on a sketchy catalogue description of condition & history. The opportunity to inspect is limited and you cannot drive the car. Auction cars are often a little below par and may require some work. It's easy to overbid. There will usually be a buyer's premium to pay in addition to the auction hammer price.

Which auction?
Auctions by established auctioneers are advertised in car magazines and on the auction houses' websites. A catalogue, or a simple printed list of the lots for auctions might only be available a day or two ahead, though often lots are listed and pictured on auctioneers' websites much earlier. Contact the auction company to ask if previous auction selling prices are available as this is useful information (details of past sales are often available on websites).

Catalogue, entry fee and payment details
When you purchase the catalogue of the vehicles in the auction, it often acts as a ticket allowing two people to attend the viewing days and the auction. Catalogue details tend to be comparatively brief, but will include information such as "one owner from new, low mileage, full service history," etc. It will also usually show a guide price to give you some idea of what to expect to pay and will tell you what is charged as a 'Buyer's premium.' The catalogue will also contain details of acceptable forms of payment. At the fall of the hammer an immediate deposit is usually required, the balance payable within 24 hours. If the plan is to pay by cash there may be a cash limit. Some auctions will accept payment by debit card. Sometimes credit or charge cards are acceptable, but will often incur an extra charge. A bank draft or bank transfer will have to be arranged in advance with your own bank as well as with the auction house. No car will be released before all payments are cleared. If delays occur in payment transfers, then storage costs can accrue.

Buyer's premium
A buyer's premium will be added to the hammer price: don't forget this in your calculations. It is not usual for there to be a further state tax or local tax on the purchase price and/or on the buyer's premium.

Viewing
In some instances it's possible to view on the day, or days before, as well as in the hours prior to, the auction. There are auction officials available who are willing to help out by opening engine and luggage compartments and to allow you to inspect the interior. While the officials may start the engine for you, a test drive is out of the question. Crawling under and around the car as much as you want is permitted, but you can't suggest that the car you are interested in be jacked up, or attempt to do the job yourself. You can also ask to see any documentation available.

Bidding

Before you take part in the auction, decide your maximum bid - and stick to it!

It may take a while for the auctioneer to reach the lot you are interested in, so use that time to observe how other bidders behave. When it's the turn of your car, attract the auctioneer's attention and make an early bid. The auctioneer will then look to you for a reaction every time another bid is made; usually the bids will be in fixed increments until the bidding slows, when smaller increments will often be accepted before the hammer falls. If you want to withdraw from the bidding, make sure the auctioneer understands your intentions - a vigorous shake of the head when he or she looks to you for the next bid should do the trick! Assuming that you are the successful bidder, the auctioneer will note your card or paddle number, and from that moment on you will be responsible for the vehicle. If the car is unsold, either because it failed to reach the reserve or because there was little interest, it may be possible to negotiate with the owner, via the auctioneers, after the sale is over.

Successful bid

There are two more items to think about. How to get the Boxster home and insurance? If you can't drive the car, your own or a hired trailer is one way; another is to have the vehicle shipped using the facilities of a local company. The auction house will also have details of companies specialising in the transfer of cars.

Insurance for immediate cover can usually be purchased on site, but it may be more cost-effective to make arrangements with your own insurance company in advance, and then call to confirm the full details.

eBay & other online auctions?

eBay & other online auctions could land you a high mileage 986 Boxster at a bargain price, though you'd be foolhardy to bid without examining the car first, something most vendors encourage. A useful feature of eBay is that the geographical location of the car is shown, so you can narrow your choices to those within a realistic radius of home. Be prepared to be outbid in the last few moments of the auction. Remember, your bid is binding and that it will be very, very difficult to get restitution in the case of a crooked vendor fleecing you – *caveat emptor*!

Be aware that some cars offered for sale in online auctions are 'ghost' cars. Don't part with any cash without being sure that the vehicle does actually exist and is as described (usually pre-bidding inspection is possible).

Auctioneers

Barrett-Jackson www.barrett-jackson.com
Bonhams www.bonhams.com
British Car Auctions (BCA) www.bca-europe.com or www.british-car-auctions.co.uk
Cheffins www.cheffins.co.uk
Christies www.christies.com
Coys www.coys.co.uk
eBay www.ebay.com
H&H www.classic-auctions.co.uk
RM www.rmauctions.com
Shannons www.shannons.com.au
Silver www.silverauctions.com

11 Paperwork
– correct documentation is essential!

The paper trail

Porsche cars usually come with a large portfolio of paperwork accumulated and passed on by a succession of proud owners. This documentation represents the real history of the car and from it can be deduced the level of care the car has received, how much it's been used, which specialists have worked on it and the dates of routine maintenance, major repairs and restorations. All of this information will be priceless to you as the new owner, so be very wary of cars with little paperwork to support their claimed history.

Registration documents

All countries/states have some form of registration for private vehicles whether its like the American 'pink slip' system or the British 'log book' system.

It is essential to check that the registration document is genuine, that it relates to the car in question, and that all the vehicle's details are correctly recorded, including chassis/VIN and engine numbers (if these are shown). If you are buying from the previous owner, his or her name and address will be recorded in the document: this will not be the case if you are buying from a dealer.

In the UK the current (Euro-aligned) registration document is named 'V5C,' and is printed in coloured sections of blue, green and pink. The blue section relates to the car specification, the green section has details of the new owner and the pink section is sent to the DVLA in the UK when the car is sold. A small section in yellow deals with selling the car within the motor trade.

Previous ownership records

Due to the introduction of important new legislation on data protection, it is no longer possible to acquire, from the British DVLA, a list of previous owners of a car you own, or are intending to purchase. This scenario will also apply to dealerships and other specialists, from who you may wish to make contact and acquire information on previous ownership and work carried out.

If the car has a foreign registration, there may be expensive and time-consuming formalities to complete. Do you really want the hassle?

Roadworthiness certificate

Most country/state administrations require that vehicles are regularly tested to prove that they are safe to use on the public highway and do not produce excessive emissions. In the UK that test (the 'MOT') is carried out at approved testing stations, for a fee. In the USA the requirement varies, but most states insist on an emissions test every two years as a minimum, while the police are charged with pulling over unsafe-looking vehicles.

In the UK the test is required on an annual basis once a vehicle becomes three years old. Of particular relevance for older cars is that the certificate issued includes the mileage reading recorded at the test date and, therefore, becomes an independent record of that car's history. Ask the seller if previous certificates are available. Without an MOT the vehicle should be trailered to its new home, unless you insist that a valid MOT is part of the deal. (Not such a bad idea this, as at least you will know the car was roadworthy on the day it was tested and you don't need to wait for the old certificate to expire before having the test done.)

In the UK, vehicles over 40 years old on May 20th each year, are exempt from MOT testing. Owners can still have the test carried out if they so wish.

Road licence

The administration of every country/state charges some kind of tax for the use of its road system, the actual form of the 'road licence' and, how it is displayed, varying enormously country to country and state to state.

Whatever the form of the road licence, it must relate to the vehicle carrying it and must be present and valid if the car is to be driven on the public highway legally.

Changed legislation in the UK means that the seller of a car must surrender any existing road fund licence, and it is the responsibility of the new owner to re-tax the vehicle at the time of purchase and before the car can be driven on the road. It's therefore vital to see the Vehicle Registration Certificate (V5C) at the time of purchase, and to have access to the New Keeper Supplement (V5C/2), allowing the buyer to obtain road tax immediately.

In the UK, classic vehicles 40 years old or more on the 1st January each year get free road tax. It is still necessary to renew the tax status every year, even if there is no change.

If the car is untaxed because it has not been used for a period of time, the owner has to inform the licensing authorities.

Certificates of authenticity

For most Porsche models it is possible to obtain a certificate proving the age and authenticity (e.g. engine and chassis numbers, paint colour and trim). If you want to obtain one, the only place to start is with your local Porsche dealer, but there is a cost involved and in some countries it's not possible to obtain a Certificate of Authenticity.

If the car has been used in European classic car rallies it may have a FIVA (Federation Internationale des Vehicules Anciens) certificate. The so-called 'FIVA Passport', or 'FIVA Vehicle Identity Card,' enables organisers and participants to recognise whether or not a particular vehicle is suitable for individual events. If you want to obtain such a certificate go to www.fbhvc.co.uk or www.fiva.org there will be similar organisations in other countries too.

Valuation certificate

Hopefully, the vendor will have a recent valuation certificate, or letter signed by a recognised expert stating how much he, or she, believes the particular car to be worth (such documents, together with photos, are usually needed to get 'agreed value' insurance). Generally such documents should act only as confirmation of your own assessment of the car rather than a guarantee of value as the expert has probably not seen the car in the flesh. The easiest way to find out how to obtain a formal valuation is to contact the owners club.

Service history

Try to obtain as much service history and other paperwork pertaining to the car as you can. Naturally, dealer stamps, or specialist garage receipts score most points in the value stakes. However, anything helps in the great authenticity game: items like the original bill of sale, handbook, parts invoices and repair bills, adding to the story and the character of the car. Even a brochure correct to the year of the car's manufacture is a useful document and something that you could well have to search hard to locate in future years. If the seller claims that the car has been restored, then expect receipts and other evidence from a specialist restorer.

If the seller claims to have carried out regular servicing, ask what work was completed, when, and seek some evidence of it being carried out. Your assessment of the car's overall condition should tell you whether the seller's claims are genuine.

Restoration photographs
If the seller tells you that the car has been restored, then expect to be shown a series of photographs taken while the restoration was under way. Pictures taken at various stages, and from various angles, should help you gauge the thoroughness of the work. If you buy the car, ask if you can have all the photographs as they form an important part of the vehicle's history. It's surprising how many sellers are happy to part with their car and accept your cash, but want to hang on to their photographs! In the latter event, you may be able to persuade the vendor to get a set of copies made.

12 What's it worth?
– let your head rule your heart

Heart and head
I believe you will know the right Porsche for you. It's the one that puts a permanent smile on your face and causes your heart to race like the first time you were in love! But this is a cruel world and you must not let your heart rule your head because, if you get it wrong, your heart will sink and that may just be the start of your troubles ...

Condition
If the car you've been looking at is really bad, then you've probably not bothered to use the marking system in chapter 9 - 60 minute evaluation. You may not have even got as far as using that chapter at all!

If you did use the marking system in chapter 9 you'll know whether the car is in excellent (maybe concours), good, average or poor condition or, perhaps, somewhere in-between these categories. Many car magazines run a regular price guide. If you haven't bought the latest editions, do so now and compare their suggested values for the model you are thinking of buying: also look at the auction prices they're reporting. Values have been fairly stable for some time, but some models will always be more sought-after than others. Trends can change too. The values published in the magazines tend to vary from one magazine to another, as do their scales of condition, so read carefully the guidance notes they provide. Bear in mind that a car that is truly a recent show winner could be worth more than the highest scale published. Assuming that the car you have in mind is not in show/concours condition, relate the level of condition that you judge the car to be in with the appropriate guide price. How does the figure compare with the asking price? Before you start haggling with the seller, consider what affect any variation from standard specification might have on the car's value. If you are buying from a dealer, remember there will be a dealer's premium (profit margin) on the price as they have to feed their families as well.

Desirable options/extras
Porsche design option package
Sport model option package
Chrono sport option packages

Undesirable features
Repainted and/or the original colour changed
Unapproved aftermarket wheels and tyres (incorrect size and offset)
Noisy aftermarket exhaust modifications
Non-Porsche aerodynamic additions

Warranty
Commercial car dealers have to provide a minimum period of warranty on certain items on any car, but in the real world is the warranty worth the paper it's written on? Look around; is this dealer capable of dealing with repairing sophisticated Porsche

engineering? What's covered by the warranty? How far from the dealer do you live? How are you going to get the car back to the dealer? What about purchasing extended warranty policies? Ask yourself the same questions. Is the company underwriting the warranty policy going to be around in two years? Warranties, unless purchasing from a reputable approved Porsche dealer, should not be a purchase consideration as, in the real world, nine out of ten times when something fails it is not going to be repaired under any warranty scheme without a fight which more often than not the buyer loses. Maybe it might be worth getting a discount on the purchase price and foregoing the warranty altogether?

Private purchases are not protected by mandatory warranty requirements and getting a previous owner to pay for undisclosed problems and any repairs usually involves legal action.

Pre-purchase inspection (PPI)

This buyer's guide contains many procedures that you as the buyer can follow, but I still strongly recommend that any 986 model being seriously considered for purchase be taken to a recognised expert, usually a Porsche dealer for a fully independent inspection. A PPI should also detect any legal issues such as forged registration papers which are becoming an ever increasing problem in the United Kingdom after the theft of hundreds of thousands of official V5 forms in 2006. Ringing of VINs or detecting clones of legally registered cars does require expertise, but nothing is ever guaranteed. You will have to pay for such an inspection, but it's worth it.

Striking a deal

Negotiate on the basis of your condition assessment, mileage and fault rectification cost. Also take into account the car's specification. Be realistic about the value, but don't be completely intractable: a small compromise on the part of the vendor or buyer will often facilitate a deal at little real cost. However, it's critical that you use your evaluation points score as your basis for negotiating the price down. If you have identified problems that from this guide or from other sources you know are going to cost a lot of money to rectify, you must insist these costs are deducted from the final purchase price. Just one failed electronic unit can cost a lot of money, so why pay for it if you already know it's failed? It's far better to walk away from a deal than to let your heart rule your head. There is always a better deal out there ... somewhere.

13 Do you really want to restore?
– it'll take longer and cost more than you think

A Porsche 986 Boxster is not a normal car. Its unibody or monocoque construction is an extremely complicated piece of design and engineering. It's very difficult to pull apart, repair and put back together *properly*. The biggest issue with structural repair is getting all the right parts, jigging and clamping them correctly into position, welding accurately and treating the metalwork, including the weld joints to ensure that rust cannot form in and around the repair during the restoration, and after it's all been painted.

Specialist tools and equipment, including a proper assembly jig will be required for all structural repairs, as will the factory workshop structural repair manual, which must be followed to the letter. There are no shortcuts when the objective is to repair a car's structure properly, and the likely need for new coolant radiators for crash-damaged cars adds to the overall complexity and cost of repair.

Standard and optional electrical, electronic and mechanical systems installed in the 986 model range are complicated, and components such as system control units extremely expensive to purchase. Damaged wiring looms are a nightmare to repair.

In summary, each of these cars is a piece of precision engineering, and does not lend itself easily to major restoration, but if you are not convinced, read on McDuff ...

Questions and answers
The biggest cost in any restoration is labour; can you do it all yourself or do you need professional help?
- How are your welding and painting skills?
- Do you have the required tooling and specialist equipment, including a monocoque jig for any structural repairs?
- Do you have the Porsche workshop structural repair manual?
- Do you have the facilities?
- Do you have an approved Porsche dealer nearby?
- Do you have the time?
- How long do you expect it to last? Your dedication is strong now, but will it still be in two years' time?
- If you cannot do the work yourself, can you afford professional restoration? A full external and internal restoration including engine and transmission rebuilds is going to cost a huge amount in any currency.
- Is a rolling chassis restoration an option? Good luck in finding one.

In theory if a full 'nut & bolt' restoration is intended it's usually best to buy the worst car you can find, so long as certain components are good, but how will you know what's good and what's not without specialist test equipment and knowledge?

Will the money ploughed into a full restoration ever be recovered? Not a chance. In the Porsche world originality is always worth more than restored.

A 986 Boxster restoration can only be approached as a labour of love as it makes no economic sense; it's actually much cheaper to buy a fully functional, higher mileage example.

It will just buff out ...
(Courtesy Ben Jones)

... maybe not. (Courtesy Ben Jones)

That's got to hurt, and, sadly, restoration
is not possible.
(Courtesy Porsche AG archive)

Serious crash damage and not a realistic
restoration project. (Courtesy Ben Jones)

... ditto ... (Courtesy Ben Jones)

... ditto. (Courtesy Ben Jones)

14 Paint problems
– bad complexion, including dimples, pimples and bubbles

Paint faults generally occur due lack of protection and/or maintenance, or to poor preparation prior to a repaint or touch-up. Some of the following conditions may be present in the car you're looking at:

Orange peel (bad)
Most Boxsters leave the factory with a slight orange peel look. However, bad orange peel is an uneven paint surface, similar to the appearance of the skin of an orange. The fault is caused by the failure of atomized paint droplets to flow into each other when they hit the surface. It's sometimes possible to rub out the effect with proprietary paint cutting/rubbing compound or very fine grades of abrasive paper. A repaint may be necessary in severe cases. Consult a bodywork repairer/paint shop for advice on the particular car.

986 Boxster in the factory paint shop ... (Courtesy Porsche AG archive)

... ditto... (Courtesy Porsche AG archive)

.. the process always resulted in a finish with a slight orange peel effect. (Courtesy Porsche AG archive)

Cracking
Severe cases are likely to have been caused by too heavy an application of paint (or filler beneath the paint). Also, insufficient stirring of the paint before application can lead to the components being improperly mixed, and cracking can result. Incompatibility of new paint with the paint already on the panel can have a similar effect. To rectify the problem it is necessary to rub down to a smooth, sound finish before repainting the problem area. Rolling of wings (fenders/guards) can also cause cracking.

Crazing
Sometimes the paint takes on a crazed rather than a cracked appearance when the problems mentioned under 'Cracking' are present. This problem can also be caused by a reaction between the underlying surface and the paint. Paint removal and repainting the problem area is usually the only solution. Painted thermal plastics will craze over time.

Blistering
Very rare, but when it does occur it's always caused by rust developing underneath

the paint. Usually perforation will be found in the metal and the damage will usually be worse than that suggested by the area of blistering. The metal will have to be repaired before repainting.

Micro blistering
Usually the result of a cheap repaint. Consult a paint specialist, but usually damaged paint will have to be removed before partial or full repaint.

Fading and oxidation
Some colours, especially solid reds, are prone to fading and oxidation if subjected to strong sunlight for long periods without constant polish protection. Sometimes proprietary paint restorers and/or paint cutting/rubbing compounds will retrieve the situation. Often a repaint is the only real solution.

Peeling
Often a problem with metallic paintwork begins when the sealing lacquer becomes damaged and begins to peel off. Poorly applied paint may also peel. The remedy is to strip and start again!

Dimples
Caused by the residue of polish (particularly silicone types) not being removed properly before repainting. Paint removal and repainting is the only solution.

Dents
Small dents are usually easily fixed by the 'Dentmaster', or equivalent process, that sucks or pushes out the dent (as long as the paint surface is still intact). Companies offering dent removal services usually come to your home: consult your telephone directory.

Look after the paint and the 986 Boxster will remain in pristine condition for years to come. (Author collection)

Some parts of the interior may be painted depending upon customer specification. (Courtesy Porsche AG archive)

Porsche interior paint schemes are also known for their durability. (Courtesy Porsche AG archive)

15 Problems due to lack of use
– just like their owners, Porsches need exercise!

Dolly Parton was asked once why she was still working as hard as ever in the music industry. She answered: "I'd rather wear out than rust out." Letting a 986 stand unused will ensure it develops some problems.

So, what can happen if a 986 is not used and just sits?

Internal corrosion

All 986 models are fitted with a wet-sump horizontally opposed six-cylinder engine meaning that, when it's switched off, most of the oil is retained inside the engine, albeit in what Porsche call an internal oil-tank. The only protection against the onset of corrosion once the engine is stationary is the oil film left on the engine's components and, if the engine remains stationary for a period of time, gravity takes over and the oil drains away and leaves areas of bare metal unprotected. Over a long period of lack of use corrosion will start on any unprotected exposed areas of bare metal, but that's not all, there's another problem. Oil starts to break down (separates into various chemical compounds). Depending on the type of oil used, some of the chemical compounds may recombine to form an acidic residue that corrodes any exposed metal it comes in contact with. Modern petrol blends with ethanol content greater than 10% will also cause internal corrosion of the fuel delivery system right up to the fuel injectors. Corroded metal fuel manifold lines will result in fuel leaks and present a real danger of fire when the engine starts.

Non-use during winter storage can create minor problems ...
(Courtesy Don Watson)

... the need to recharge a flat battery being one of them.
(Author collection)

Seized components

Pistons in brake callipers will seize du to corrosion as the dust caps and seals dry out, crack and fail.

Moisture in the brake fluid which is used in many systems will start internal system corrosion. The main components affected are: the brake master cylinder, clutch slave cylinder and ABS hydraulic unit. If the internals have corroded, it's quite possible that horrendous problems will occur when the Boxster is started.

Steel brake discs (rotors) rust and the brake pads may also stick to them.

The clutch may seize if the plate becomes stuck to the flywheel because of corrosion. Hand brakes (emergency/parking brake) will seize as cables and linkages rust. In the 986 series the handbrake assembly is installed in the rear wheel hubs, old technology, quite complicated and yes, expensive to repair.

Internal seals

Without fluid for lubrication even synthetic rubber seals will start to dry out and break down. The 986 engine series all use large numbers of o-rings and gaskets, long term storage without due care and attention will result in many oil leaks once it's started again. The same issue applies in the braking system.

External seals

As time passes all the rubber sealing used to protect the car against water ingress will harden, crack and fail.

Fluids

Old acidic engine oil will corrode any exposed metal it can get to. Brake fluid absorbs water from the atmosphere and must be renewed every two years.

Untreated water left in the windscreen (windshield) washer system will stagnate.

Tyres & wheels

Tyres that have had the weight of the car on them in a single position for some time will develop flat spots, resulting in driving vibrations. The tyre walls may develop cracks or (blister-type) bulges and aged rubber (over 6 years) can become too hard and unsafe.

Corroded wheels are expensive to repair and/or replace.

MacPherson struts & shock absorbers (dampers)

With lack of use damper seals will fail allowing the gas used as part of the internal damping system to escape and they will collapse.

Rubber & plastic

Rubber is used throughout the car in various mounts for the transmission and suspension and in bushings and once it goes hard and cracks all sorts of grunts, groans, vibrations and in the worst case scenario handling problems can occur.

Fuel hoses are made from rubber as are many of the engine oil system interconnects. Once these hoses perish there is a serious risk of fire.

Halfshaft (driveshaft) CV joints and steering arms have rubber covers (boots) and when they crack it allows the outside environment into sensitive lubricated components which will eventually fail.

Electrics

Leaving a battery installed and not driving the car can result it going completely flat in less than four weeks and in winter it will die faster. A lead acid battery left discharged for long periods of time will not be capable of being recharged and will have to be replaced.

Exhaust system

Exhaust gas always contains water. Water sitting for long periods of time in a cold exhaust system will cause it to rot from the inside. The outside of the exhaust system will also rust due to corrosive elements in the atmosphere or salt and other road grime that becomes stuck to it.

Mould

Most of the 986 model range is fitted with a full leather interior. Given the right environmental conditions, moisture inside the car will result in mould growing on the leather, and spreading throughout the entire interior.

Mould will ruin leather. Take care to protect the interior against mould when the car is in storage, even if it's only for a short time, but especially in moist environments.
(Courtesy Bob Schoenherr)

16 The Community
– key people, organisations and companies in the Boxster's world

This chapter provides various sources any prospective 986 Boxster owner can seek advice and guidance from, what's available to read and which organisations to join if a purchase is made.

Books
Porsche Boxster The Complete Story by Gavin Farmer, published by The Crowood Press, ISBN: 1-86126-675-8 and 978-1-861266-75-0.

Porsche Boxster Service Manual: 1997-2004 Boxster, Boxster S, published by Bentley Publishers, ISBN: 0837613337 and 978-0-837613-33-8.

Magazines
There is no specific Porsche 986 Boxster magazine. However, in many Porsche club magazines the 986 Boxster and its owners frequently appear in print and often have dedicated sections/experts.

Porsche major assembly rebuild and/or exchange services
Note that regional and national clubs will also be able to provide details of specialists in your part of the world.

Autofarm (1973) Ltd
Oddington Grange
Weston-on-the-Green
Oxfordshire
OX25 3QW
England
Tel: +44 (0)1865 331234
www.autofarm.co.uk

Sportec AG
Hofstrasse 17
CH-8181 Höri bei Bülach/ZH
Switzerland
Tel: +41 (0) 43 411 43 00
www.sportec.ch

Porsche parts suppliers
Porsche Centre Hatfield
1 Hatfield Avenue
Hatfield Business Park
Hatfield
Hertfordshire
AL10 9UA,
England

Tel: +44 (0) 1707 277911
www.porschehost.com/home.asp?opc=hatfield

Porsch-Apart Ltd
Unit 4 Field Mill
Harrison Street
Ramsbottom
Bury
Lancashire
BL0 0AH
England
Tel: +44 (0) 1706 824053
www.porsch-apart.co.uk

Porsche clubs
The author has been involved with some UK and European based Porsche clubs in the past and is happy to recommend:

http://www.porscheclubgb.com/
Porsche Club Great Britain Registered office
Cornbury House
Cotswold Business Village, London Road
Moreton-in-Marsh
Gloucestershire
GL56 0JQ
England
Tel: +44 (0)1608 652911

http://www.tipec.net/ (The Independent Porsche Enthusiasts Club)
TIPEC Club Office
10 Whitecroft Gardens
Woodford Halse
Northants
NN11 3PY
England
Tel: +44 (0) 8456 020052

Internet-based Porsche communities
For North American readers please check with the Porsche Club America website www.pca.org to find the contact address of the PCA region nearest to you.

Google is your friend. Use the search words 'Porsche 986' 'Boxster' to get started or check out:

http://www.iwantaporsche.net/ interesting website by a Porsche Boxster owner.
http://www.ppbb.com/board/main.htm Porsche Boxster specific website.
http://www.986faq.com/ Porsche 986 Boxster specific website.

Production numbers

Model year	Model	Number manufactured
1997	Boxster 2.5-litre	15,790
1998	Boxster 2.5-litre	17,086
1999	Boxster 2.5-litre	22,829
2000	Boxster 2.7-litre	14,599
	Boxster S 3.2-litre	11,467
2001	Boxster 2.7-litre	14,000
	Boxster S 3.2-litre	14,457
2002	Boxster 2.7 litre	11,608
	Boxster S 3.2-litre	10,381
2003	Boxster 2.7-litre	10,284
	Boxster S 3.2-litre	8504
2004	Boxster 2.7-litre	6615
	Boxster S 3.2-litre	4621
	Boxster Spyder	1964*
2005	Boxster 2.7-litre	426
	Boxster S 3.2-litre	243

Note: Total 986 Boxster and Boxster S including the Boxster Spyder (*all but one built in Finland) production totalled 164,874. Of these 108,772 were built by Valmet in Finland.

Engine specifications

Engine type:	M96.20	M96.22 M96.23	M96.21 M96.24
Bore mm (in)	85.5 (3.37)	85.5 (3.37)	93 (3.66)
Stroke mm (in)	72 (2.83)	78 (3.07)	
Displacement cc (cu.in)	2480 (151.34)	2687 (163.96)	3179 (193.98)
Compression ratio	11.0:1		
Horsepower (Kw/hp)@rpm	150/204@6000	160/218@6300 MY00 162/220@6300 MY01 168/225@6300 MY03	185/252@6200 MY00 191/258@6200 MY03
Torque (Nm/ft-lb)@rpm	245/181@4500	260/192@4700	310/229@4600
Maximum rpm	6700	7200	
Fuel octane	95 to 98 RON (90 to 93 CLC or AKI) premium unleaded		
Fuel consumption L/100km (mpg)	8-11L 100km (21-27mpg)		
Oil press@5000 rpm (oil temp. 90°C/194°F)	6.5 bar (94psi)		
Oil consumption	1.5 litres per 1000km (1.59 US quarts per 621 miles)		

Transmission types

Designation	Model year(s)	Type and model application
G86.00	1997 to 1999	5-speed manual for 2.5L Boxster
A86.00	1997 to 1999	5-speed Tiptronic S for 2.5L Boxster
G86.01	2000 to 2005	5-speed manual for 2.7L Boxster
A86.05	2000 to 2005	5-speed Tiptronic S for 2.7L Boxster
G86.20	2000 to 2005	6-speed Tiptronic S for 3.2L Boxster S
A86.20	2000 to 2005	5-speed Tiptronic S for 3.2L Boxster S

Note: A limited slip differential was not offered as standard or as an option for any Porsche 986 Boxster model and/or transmission.

Brake system specifications

986 Boxster Model	Boost system	Front callipers / Rear callipers	Steel front discs (rotors) / Steel rear discs (rotors)	Ceramic front discs (rotors) / Ceramic rear discs (rotors)
All	Vacuum	4-piston black	Vented/perforated	N/A
		4-piston black	Vented/perforated	

Note: The 986 Boxster is delivered as standard with the 3-channel ABS 5.3 system. As an option the 4-channel ABS/TC 5.3 system was available, which consisted of: individual wheel ABS, Traction control (TC), ASR (anti-slip control) and ABD (automatic brake differential). From model year 2001 the Porsche stability management (PSM) system was also made available as an option. PSM was fitted as standard to special models such as the Boxster S 550 Spyder 50th Anniversary Edition.

Dimensions

986 Boxster model & model years	Length mm (inches)	Width mm (inches)	Roof height mm (inches)
Boxster	4340 (170.8)	1780 (70.1)	1290 (50.8)
Boxster S	4340 (170.8)	1780 (70.1)	1290 (50.8)
Boxster S 550 Spyder	4340 (170.8)	1780 (70.1)	1290 (50.8)

Empty weights

986 model	*Weight range kg (lb)
Boxster 2.5L with manual transmission	1239 to 1382 (2732 to 3046)
Boxster 2.5L with Tiptronic transmission	1291 to 1677 (2847 to 3698)
Boxster 2.7L with manual transmission	1275 to 1400 (2811 to 3086)
Boxster 2.7L with Tiptronic transmission	1330 to 1727 (2932 to 3808)
Boxster 3.2L with manual transmission	1320 to 1430 (2910 to 3153)
Boxster S 3.2L with Tiptronic transmission	1360 to 1470 (2998 to 3241)

Note: Specific delivered car weight is totally option dependent.

Approved tyres

Porsche approved and tested tyres for the complete 986 Boxster model range		
Wheel diameter	**Brand and type**	**N rating**
16 inch	Pirelli P-Zero Directionale	N3
	Michelin Pilot Exalto PE2	N0
	Bridgestone Potenza S-02	N3
	Continental ContiSportContact	N1
	Michelin SX MXX3	N2
	Pirelli P-Zero Assimetrico	N3
	Bridgestone Expedia S-01	N2
	Bridgestone Expedia S-02	N3
	Michelin Pilot Sport PS2	N3
17 inch	Pirelli P-Zero Rosso	N3
	Bridgestone Potenza S-02A	N4
	Continental ContiSportContact2	N2
	Michelin Pilot Sport PS2	N3
	Pirelli Winter W240 Snowsport	N1
18 inch	Pirelli P-Zero Rosso	N3
	Bridgestone Potenza S-02A	N4
	Continental ContiSportContact2	N2
	Michelin Pilot Sport PS2	N3
	Dunlop SP 9090	N0
	Pirelli P-Zero Rosso	N4
	Pirelli Winter W240 Snowsport	N1

www.velocebooks.com / www.veloce.co.uk
Details of all current books • New book news • Special offers

Also from Veloce Publishing –

Paperback • 28x21cm
• 640 pages • 1300 b&w pictures
ISBN: 978-1-787115-50-7

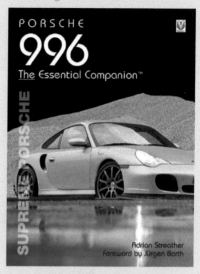

Paperback • 28x21cm
• 656 pages • 1545 pictures
ISBN: 978-1-845849-54-2

Paperback • 28x21cm
• 704 pages • 1500 pictures
• ISBN: 978-1-845846-20-6

Paperback • 28x21cm
• 432 pages • 1180 pictures
• ISBN: 978-1-845849-55-9

For more info on Veloce titles, visit our website at www.veloce.co.uk
email: info@veloce.co.uk • Tel: +44(0)1305 260068

The Essential Buyer's Guide™ series ...

For more details visit: www.veloce.co.uk
email: info@veloce.co.uk
tel: 01305 260068

Index